SOUL STORM

ED OLIVO

SOUL STORM

When The Journey Is The Destination

Charleston, SC
www.PalmettoPublishing.com

SoulStorm

Copyright © 2021 by Ed Olivo

All rights reserved
No portion of this book may be reproduced,
stored in a retrieval system, or transmitted
in any form by any means–electronic, mechanical,
photocopy, recording, or other–except for brief
quotations in printed reviews, without prior
permission of the author.

First Edition

Paperback ISBN: 978-1-63837-350-6
eBook ISBN: 978-1-63837-351-3

TABLE OF CONTENTS

Gratitude and Dedications vii

Foreword ix

Part One: Whim and Wonder—The Quickening 1
The Love Letter / Her / Our Place / Her Needs / What I'll Give Her / Insensibility / Backpack of Forgotten Dreams / Molten Starlight / Impossibly / A Feather's Breath / Colors / Sparks of Eternity / A Rainbow's Dance / The Shift / A Drop of Everything / The Fires of Love / My Beautiful Invader / The Heart of Beauty / Why Time Is Meaningless / Eternity in a Moment / When It Happened / Music to My Ears / A Question / Perfect Vision / Lost / The Wonder of Wandering / The Reason Why

Part Two: Chaos and Descent—The Storm 13
Soulstorm / Wondrous Melancholy / Tormented Angel / StormChild / StormDancer / Pathway / My Horizon / Longing / You / Snowdrift / The Stand / Her Voice / The Storm / The Storm's Path / Sorrowful Knowledge / Sweet Pain / What Should Have Been

Part Three: Awakening and Acceptance—The Calm 21
Solace / Blissful Weariness / Light / Messages / Steps / Commitment / All In / Strength / Relentless / A Moment / Healing / Three Things / Flow / Belief / An Ending and a Beginning

Final Thoughts 27

GRATITUDE AND DEDICATIONS

First and foremost, all glory and thanks to God above…the only One who has been with me for every step of my life thus far.

I'd like to thank and dedicate this book to the following people:

My daughter, Angelica…my angel, my hero, my inspiration

My beautiful, supportive family

My friends who kept me encouraged throughout the process

And you…because you matter so very much

FOREWORD

This is a book about love.

This is not a typical book about love because, well, there is no typical sort of experience with love.

I believe that love is the only perfect force in this world. How each one of us experiences that power is singular and unique to every one of us.

Yes, there are certain universal emotions that help us to relate to, and share in, each other's experiences—joy, warmth, pain, sadness, loneliness, anger, fear, and so on. But how these emotions help shape our own love is what makes each of our journeys so special and incomparable to any other.

So I consider this to be a collection of my own experiences, thoughts, and whims. A twisting, glorious, still-happening journey that I would like to share with you.

As we walk together, we may or may not agree on some things, and that's OK. Companionship is really about respect and understanding anyway. And I don't need to personally know you to respect and open myself up to understanding you…love taught me that.

I can tell you that it will be messy and beautiful, painful and wonderful, confusing and illuminating.

There will be sunshine and warmth, but also lots of foul, miserable weather. We'll find some rest and shelter along the way, in the in-between places of our hearts and souls…but not much. Because ultimately, it is exposure to the various elements, good and bad, that will allow us to relate to each other and connect. That's what sharing is…love taught me that.

Are you ready? I hope so, because a storm is coming. But I promise you this: you won't go through it alone. I'll be right by your side, and you'll be by mine. And that's all that matters.

Love taught me that too.

PART ONE
WHIM AND
WONDER—THE QUICKENING

The Love Letter

Dear Promised One,

Hi, it's me. We've never actually met, but still, I miss you.

I'll be sitting here, waiting.

Take your time...I've got forever, and when you bring yours with you, we'll have plenty of time.

Don't worry; I have a book to read and one to write.

I've read the one a thousand times, it's the story of you...of us...of this.

Oh, and it's the same one I'm writing, so I'll keep myself busy.

I've got music too.

The melody of your voice rings softly and unendingly throughout my core.

And I have a music player.

I have some cookies to eat and share with you; I hope you like them.

I'll be waiting by the tree our souls planted a thousand years ago.

You know the one…the tree our names are carved into with the

strained ink of past broken hearts, shattered hopes, and painful moments.

I'll see you soon.

I love you…I truly do.

Her

She smiled, and the sun went dim.
  She wept, and oceans dried.
  She laughed, and music faded.
  She whispered, and thunder was silenced.
  She dreamed, and worlds collided.
  She awoke, and I fell into a dream.
  Who is she?

Our Place

I dreamed of her and a place that only we could travel to.

A place of colors and textures and layers and beautiful, delightful chaos.

A place I miss with the force of a soulstorm.

Her Needs

She didn't need a new story…she wanted someone who desired to read hers.
　She didn't want someone to change her…she longed for someone to accept her.
　She didn't require a new path…she ached for someone to walk on hers, by her side.
　She didn't need a hero…she just wanted to be saved.

What I'll Give Her

She longs for the moon, so I'll give her the night.
　She needs to see; my love blinds her sight.
　She wants to stay and be never apart.
　She wants it all, so I'll give her my heart.

Insensibility

She defied the senses.
　Around her, colors carried a redolence unknown, sweet and pure.
　Near her, I could feel her soul breathing and the eternity of her love.
　In her arms, I heard the delicate sound of moons rising across planes and galaxies.
　She was an impossibility and impossible to love…
　So I will love her impossibly.

Backpack of Forgotten Dreams

We strolled beneath a galaxy of crimson blooms that danced joyfully in the soothing breeze.

I had a backpack full of battered memories and forgotten dreams slung over one shoulder, one that somehow grew lighter with each step we took together.

She held my hand tightly, wordlessly relaying tender but relentless waves of love and care through her fingertips.

We walked that way for two eternities without tiring.

And we kept walking.

Molten Starlight

Her beauty was natural…soft and compelling.

When she spoke, the vibrations of her delicate voice floated through my being like drifting flower petals.

When she touched my hand, it was a tempest of swirling colors and warming light.

And when we held each other, we walked upon light, and our hearts danced among the planets.

Her kiss? Molten starlight.

Impossibly

We wandered for a while, and she stopped for a moment, turning to me.
"How much do you love me?"
I cradled her chin in one hand and gently kissed an eyelid, feeling the soft pulse of her life kiss me back.
Then I whispered,
"I love you impossibly."

A Feather's Breath

She sat with me in silence as we let our hearts speak for a while.
She put her head on my shoulder and sighed beautifully, a sound of pure contentment, a feather's breath.
I heard nature's whisper, and I looked up. The trees had bloomed, each petal quiet and waiting, eager for the sound of her voice.

Colors

She loved colors and longed to twirl in new hues and shades.
I took her hand and placed it over my heart, telling her, "Feel the love that comes from the core of who I am."
She closed her eyes and smiled, exhaling softly.
And new colors appeared.

Sparks of Eternity

It was the soft sound of her breath, like the tender sigh of a rose petal unfurling in the sun.

It was the tinsel gleam in her eye when she looked at me and smiled, a moondrop of wonder and life.

Did I mention her voice? A sound of such harmony and bliss! If stars found voice, they would yet stay silent for fear of missing even the briefest utterance from her.

And so we sat under a blanket of blooms, looking over the water. She would be with me for only a short while, but we knew how to make the moments last like frozen sparks of eternity.

A Rainbow's Dance

When I awoke in her arms, I couldn't help but smile. She had changed everything.

I watched her sleep as I listened to her soothing breaths intermingle with the sound of the raindrops tapping gently on the roof.

I looked out of the window and saw a glorious, magnificent rainbow. Then I looked back at her, realizing, *Why look at the rainbow when all of life's colors are right next to you?*

The Shift

She looked at me and smiled, and my world shifted.
My heart burst into a million more hearts, each one a universe.
A sunbeam reached out to her, and she walked over to it.
She stood in the sunlight and I swear, the sun brightened and grew warmer when she did.

A Drop of Everything

Every part of you, even the most subtle…
especially the most subtle…
is like a petal of light,
a shard of eternity,
a perfect, single dewdrop of everything.

The Fires of Love

Our love was strange and overwhelming, as true love should be.
It was a fire that did not destroy—rather, one that purified.
It cleansed because the passion itself was purity unsullied and without deception or doubt…
just a raw love that grew beautiful things.

My Beautiful Invader

She approached with care.
    She attacked with hope.
    She conquered with faith.
    She occupies with love.
    She transforms all with light.
    My beautiful invader.

The Heart of Beauty

She asked if I thought she was beautiful.
    "Dear God, no!" I replied.
    She pouted.
    I smiled and explained.
    "You are this…thing, this creature that goes so far beyond our
    capacity to understand what true beauty is.
    Flowers, sunsets, and sunrises…these are beautiful.
    You…you are an unimaginable idea come to life.
    A dream from someplace where stars are birthed
    and light is formed from mists of hope and love.
    Beautiful? No, my love.
    You are the heart of true beauty."
    She looked at me, smiled, and brushed a tear from her eye.
    Then she frowned and poked me in the chest.
    "Did you just call me a thing?"
    I sighed and laughed and kissed her.
    She was perfect.

Why Time Is Meaningless

Time was meaningless to us because forever would never be enough anyway.

So we measured everything through the pulse in our veins,

as set by the joyful peaks and empty chasms of our heartbeats.

This mattered so much more than any amount of time yearned for or gifted to us.

Eternity in a Moment

While she slept in my arms, I breathed in the absolute perfectness of it all.

It was then that I realized that this divine sliver of time, this flawless "now," was infinite…

eternity in a moment.

When It Happened

I remember the precise moment it happened, that instant my heart grew wings and took me to places unknown but long-yearned for.

We were walking along a path lined by graceful, reverent trees. The bursts of sunlight that dappled the branches were daystars.

She slipped her hand into mine, and that was it. I felt something break within me, like a seed that had sprouted out of its shell. It was something beautiful and golden, and at that moment, my past made sense, my present mattered, and my future began.

Music to My Ears

There was the moving silence that only nature could orchestrate…

the soft rustle of a cooling breeze dancing around and tickling the leaves…

the melodious chirp of joyful birds exchanging notes of love and playfulness…

and the soothing sound of her voice, turning everything golden with each beautiful word.

A Question

We sat under the tree, and she looked at me with a tender frown.

"Why do you love me?" she asked in a delicate voice that coaxed the branches above to bloom, as well as my heart.

I took one of her small hands into both of my scarred ones, and I kissed her palm.

I smiled up at her and whispered, "Because I was created solely to love you."

Perfect Vision

With her, I reveled in the unbelievable…
 sky rivers…
 Earth angels…
 true love.
 Blinded by love? Perhaps…but what I see with her when we are together is all I need to see anyway.

Lost

We sat down, tired, but oh, so content.
 We were lost, but we'd never felt more at home.

The Wonder of Wandering

We looked one way and then the other. We shrugged and smiled.
 Then, after placing her hand in mine, she said, "Does it really matter which way? As long as we are together, we are exactly where we should be."

The Reason Why

She whispered three words to me.
 The sacred prayer between hearts in love.
 My heart responded with the same three words.
 Our bond was completed.
 I'd finally found the answer to all of my "whys."

PART TWO
CHAOS AND DESCENT—THE STORM

Soulstorm

There was something massive on the horizon.
Something hurtful and hungry and shredding.
A soulstorm.
And I wasn't ready.

Wondrous Melancholy

We had been walking side by side silently, lost in, and with, each other.
She looked up at the moon, and I saw a silvery tear glide down her cheek. My heart ached, a feeling of such impending loss that I couldn't stop the sob that escaped me.
She looked at me, placed a hand on my cheek, and in a voice that was like gentle rainfall over rose petals, she said, "Our time together isn't calculated by the

passing of minutes. No, my love, ours is measured by the infinite bursts of sweet light that will forever fill our hearts."

Then she vanished, and I was left small and alone.

Tormented Angel

Today, the soothing rain became a pounding torrent.
Today, the warming sun became a scalding firestorm.
Today, the gentle breeze became a raging whirlwind.
Today, the birds' joyful trill became a manic choir of impending sorrow.
Today, my angel wept, reached out to me, and faded away.

StormChild

She looked ahead, unclasped my hand, and then turned back to look at me, smiling.
"Do not fear the rain, for I am the water.
Do not fear the wind, for I am the air.
Do not fear the lightning, for I am its energy.
Now, watch how I love you!"
And with a kiss and a laugh, she flew into the storm.

StormDancer

I looked ahead and felt something hollow and cold yawn within me. The oncoming storm was massive, and it was going to hurt.

She was next to me again.

Her hand grasped mine, and a wave of reassuring warmth washed over me. Her voice glided through me, its whispery wings enveloping my tired heart.

"My love is bigger."

She kissed me, laughed and in a flash of iridescence, danced high into the swirling tempest.

Pathway

Somewhere along the way, in between the drawn breath of a whisper and a kiss, she disappeared again.

I walked on, miserable. The trees provided me some comfort, their low branches nearly brushing my shoulders, as if in compassion and understanding… do they not perpetually mourn the loss of the warmth from their fallen leaves?

I looked up and saw a soft glow in the crook of the path ahead.

I smiled. I knew she was close.

My Horizon

She was gone, and I was left with a soul filled with memories and a heart heavy with unrealized hopes.

I didn't want to walk anymore, so I sat on the side of the road and wept silently, bitter and tired.

Then, her voice…a sound that strummed my desires with beautiful song.

"Eyes upward and faith forward, my sweet…I am the horizon, and I am waiting for you."

Longing

My soul seethed, and my heart burst in longing for you.

You cannot grasp the depth nor force of how much I miss you.

You

Sometimes the emptiness gnaws at my soul and claws at my heart, a famished, angry beast.

I mourn for embraces long faded and weep for kisses that no longer have taste.

But then…you.

Peace cloaks me in warmth and comfort and golden hope.

Just you.

Snowdrift

She was with me.

Though we walked in silence, my soul heard everything she felt.

I whispered, "You're my favorite person in all of the worlds."

Then smiling joyfully, eyes glimmering with brilliant tears, she let go of my hand and melted into the pure snow, leaving me alone again.

It wasn't time.

The Stand

Alone, but not lonely.

Broken, but not beaten.

Shadows beckon, but pure light embraces me.

I stand for love.

I stand for us.

Her Voice

The darkness was enveloping, a horrid wave of engulfing anguish,

a shroud for my torment.

I could not find her.

I felt lost, and the last sliver of hope I carried pierced into my heart.

A golden needle, bright and sharp,

slowing the pain to steaming drops of melancholic memories that seared my soul.

Then…her voice…her sweet, life-filled voice.

A sound so beautiful I sobbed aloud, and that thin beam of hope exploded into a soulstorm.

Three words she spoke, and a lighted path appeared…

"I am near."

The Storm

Her kiss was lightning, quickening my pulse and energizing my senses.

Her whisper was a gale of force, blowing through my soul, scouring and cleansing.

Her embrace was like soothing, pounding rain on my love-fevered heart.

She was the storm I never wanted to end, only longing to be overwhelmed by her.

The Storm's Path

My love for you shreds and consumes me,
   but I don't mind,
   because I know what is on the other side of the storm.

Sorrowful Knowledge

I looked into her eyes and fell inside, floating peacefully in her liquid gaze.

She smiled, and I felt a starburst of colors explode within my soul, washing away doubt and fear.

I closed my eyes, and a tear streamed down my face, a tear that carried sorrowful knowledge.

I opened them again, and she was gone.

Sweet Pain

We sat for a while, being silly and nonsensical, which makes perfect sense if you've ever been in love.

Then the end of the day's eternity was upon us; it was time to part for a time.

We embraced tightly, and she kissed me soulfully.

Then she slapped me, not too hard, but enough to feel it.

I touched my face where she hit me, and I laughed in slight pain and asked why.

She said, "So the kiss tastes sweeter."

Then she giggled and flew away.

What Should Have Been

It's like arriving at your destination after a long, pain-filled, and treacherous journey, only to find an empty house because she's moved on.

So what to do?

Spend the night in the house to rest.

Only…you can't rest because there are signs and keepsakes of her everywhere.

A hair clip left on the bathroom counter.

Her favorite chipped mug in the kitchen sink.

The book she loves lying on an end table by the sofa.

So you go to the bedroom and lie down.

But it's worse.

The mattress has formed to her shape, so you lie in the curves of her ghostly presence.

The pillow smells like her favorite conditioner.

You sleep restlessly, dreaming of what might have been…what should have been.

The next morning, you get up, wipe the tears, and take a deep breath.

You shoulder your backpack; it's heavier today.

You open the door and walk to the road.

You look back at the house once more, a bittersweet representation of yet another unfulfilled dream.

You close your eyes and allow that last tear to run down your face, desperate to escape the torment in your heart and mind.

Then you turn around and keep walking, because that's all you can do.

PART THREE
AWAKENING AND ACCEPTANCE—THE CALM

Solace

The colors and sounds were soothing, even healing.

The soft laughter of the dancing, playful brook.

The solemn and stoic strength of the trees, arms raised in praise.

The wisps of lonely mist, searching longingly for an embrace that cannot last.

And a blanket of fallen leaves on the ground, sheltering the small and the lost.

Blissful Weariness

I was weary.

The truth is, I'd been walking for an awful long time and had only experienced brief moments with her alongside me.

But those moments were eternal.

I closed my eyes, and she was there.

I smiled and soaked her in.

In her presence, my soul always felt like how I imagined a flower must feel the very first time it felt the warmth of the sun.

My heart's hand clasped hers.

I smiled and walked on.

Light

I was in dark,
> and you were the light.
> You brought me the day,
> when I was lost in the night.

Messages

I spoke these words upon the wind, hoping they would find her: "When we are finally together, you will know."

I heard a feather's whisper drifting on a soft wave as it lapped against my tired feet. "What will I know?"

I smiled and whispered back, "You will know the depth of my love and commitment to you. That you are no longer alone in your journey, and that changes everything."

Steps

I was alone again, the memory of her still fragrant in my soul and pulsing through my lips. She had vanished between a breath and a blink.

I stopped at the foot of the bridge and paused, eyes glistening in longing.

Then I remembered something she had told me: "You make the journey worth every step."

So I smiled, wiped my eyes, grabbed the railing, and walked on.

Commitment

Lean on me.
 Trust me.
 Believe me.
 I will fight for you always.
 We will win.
 I am with you.

All In

Too much…I love you too much.
 But that's OK, because honestly,
 that's how I want to love you, and really, I know no other way.

Strength

Each shard of my broken heart still beats,
    each a small bloom of hopeful light.
    And when it starts to mend and her warmth binds these pulses of life and love together,
    my heart will be a garden of light and will be stronger…
    I will be stronger.

Relentless

Her love is relentless, and mine is unstoppable.
    And when we finally find each other again,
    our worlds will be reborn in the fires of that powerful, cleansing love.
    We will set the cosmos ablaze.

A Moment

Here's the thing…
    it just takes that one special moment.
    That one fraction in time when something or someone touches your heart,
    pierces through the darkness, and actually sheds a ray of light and warmth
    where there was once none.
    And then everything changes.
    It only takes a moment…

Healing

She did not tend to the scars in and on my heart.
    She simply filled the wounds with the essence of
    her love and formed binding seams of light.

Three Things

Someone to hold.
    Laughter.
    A horizon to chase.

Flow

I sleep and dream.
    I awake and walk.
    I walk and see.
    I see and learn.
    I learn and do.
    I do and grow.
    I grow and love.
    I love and live.

Belief

I believe in love.
    The fairytale kind.
    The movie kind.

The unbelievable kind.
The impossible kind.
The breathtaking kind.
The life-changing kind.
And just as importantly…
love believes in me.

An Ending and a Beginning

I wondered if it was all just my own imagination and desire.

But even if it was, it was OK.

I had learned and grown.

Love had always been inside of me, waiting to be uncovered and discovered through trial, joy, and loss.

I smiled down at the road and then looked up.

I saw the tree, massive, scarred, and beautiful.

She was sitting under it.

It was really her.

She looked up and saw me.

She stood up and smiled and reached her arms out to me, weeping with joy.

I ran to her.

FINAL THOUGHTS

So there it is…wonderfully messy and painfully beautiful, this journey. Did his journey end after he finally met her? No, not even close…he's about to realize that despite everything he's already been through, the real journey is about to begin, and it will be something fantastic and magical.

Now, maybe some of the order was wrong, or perhaps something didn't make sense. But that's how life's journeys normally are, especially the long, life-changing ones. They don't always follow a schedule or a plan or even sense, and that's fine.

It's OK to go with the flow…but always flow in a positive direction and with some ability to maneuver what you can control.

It's OK to not always follow a schedule or timelines…life doesn't, and neither does love.

It's OK to not always know what the next step is… if you move forward, even just a little bit at a time, the way becomes more clear naturally and on its own.

And we don't always carry umbrellas or are near shelter when the storms hit. Yet it's being vulnerable to the torrent that uncovers what really matters…painfully scouring, but blessedly cleansing. The soulstorm.

I'm still walking my journey, and I can't even tell you which stage I'm at right now. But what I do know is that the deepest, most important love I've encountered was the one that exposed the golden seed of love inside of me, the one that exists within all of us.

And I think that's the thing…journeys are beginnings, middles, and endings all bundled up in moments, encounters, and experiences. A lifelong process where you discover that beyond is just another beginning and that new horizons are constantly appearing before you.

Thank you for sharing part of my journey with me. I'm sincerely grateful to not have to walk alone the whole way. And who knows? Maybe parts of our journeys aren't all that different…I kind of hope they aren't, because that's what helps us connect with each other.

The journey: a process of discovery and preparation for the stops along the way, good and bad.

And that's why, often, the journey is the destination.

ABOUT THE AUTHOR

Ed Olivo lived for 23 years in Hong Kong, where he worked as a freelance journalist and published countless articles.

His deepest desire is to share and help, whenever, wherever, and with whomever he can.

He hopes to open a non-profit bookstore café that features the works of under-represented people and those who suffer from depression or anxiety, or struggle with current or past trauma. He would love to provide a platform and community where they can freely and positively express themselves while feeling supported, encouraged, and included.

Ed Olivo is the single father of an incredible daughter. He currently lives in Colorado and enjoys reading, writing, movies, sports, and video games, but above all, he most enjoys spending time with his daughter.

www.ingramcontent.com/pod-product-compliance
Ingram Content Group UK Ltd.
Pitfield, Milton Keynes, MK11 3LW, UK
UKHW022234230426
12048UKWH00018BA/1256